AF598717

Beautiful Birds

PARROTS

By Kristen Rajczak Nelson

Please visit our website, www.garethstevens.com. For a free color catalog of all our high-quality books, call toll free 1-800-542-2595 or fax 1-877-542-2596.

Library of Congress Cataloging-in-Publication Data

Names: Rajczak Nelson, Kristen, author.
Title: Parrots / by Kristen Rajczak Nelson.
Description: New York : Gareth Stevens Publishing, [2023] | Series: Beautiful birds | Includes index.
Identifiers: LCCN 2021035980 (print) | LCCN 2021035981 (ebook) | ISBN 9781538275207 (set) | ISBN 9781538275214 (library binding) | ISBN 9781538275191 (paperback) | ISBN 9781538275221 (ebook)
Subjects: LCSH: Parrots–Juvenile literature.
Classification: LCC QL696.P7 R35 2023 (print) | LCC QL696.P7 (ebook) | DDC 598.7/1–dc23
LC record available at https://lccn.loc.gov/2021035980
LC ebook record available at https://lccn.loc.gov/2021035981

First Edition

Published in 2023 by
Gareth Stevens Publishing
29 East 21st Street
New York, NY 10010

Editor: Kristen Nelson
Designer: Andrea Davison-Bartolotta

Photo credits: Cover Ondrej Prosicky/Shutterstock.com; p. 1 Napachara Tochaona/Shutterstock.com; p. 5 Cavan-Images/Shutterstock.com; pp. 7, 24 (toes) Gleb Aitov/Shutterstock.com; p. 9 (top right) Zeehan Ahmed/ Shutterstock.com; p. 9 (top left) Donatas Dabravolskas/Shutterstock.com; p. 9 (bottom right) Bappa Pabitra/ Shutterstock.com; p. 9 (bottom left) Gabriela Beres/Shutterstock.com; p. 11 Alan Jeffery/Shutterstock.com; pp. 13, 24 (rain forest) Fireflycreative/Shutterstock.com; p. 15 Reto Buhler/Shutterstock.com; p. 17 narikan/ Shutterstock.com; pp. 19, 24 (beak) Natalia Johnson/Shutterstock.com; p. 21 Valerija Polakovska/ Shutterstock.com; p. 23 Kurit afshen/Shutterstock.com.

Printed in the United States of America

CPSIA compliance information: Batch #CSGS23: For further information contact Gareth Stevens, New York, New York at 1-800-542-2595.

Contents

Parrots are birds.
They can be green.
They can be red
or blue.

They have curved beaks
They have four toes.

There are more than 300 kinds.

Macaws are some of the largest.

They live in all over the world.
They like rain forests.

They eat nuts
and seeds.
They eat fruit.

They are kept as pets.
They live at zoos too.

They are smart birds.
Some can copy speech.

They live a long time.
Some live 80 years!

They are pretty birds!

Words to Know

beak

rain forest

toes

Index

AF598732

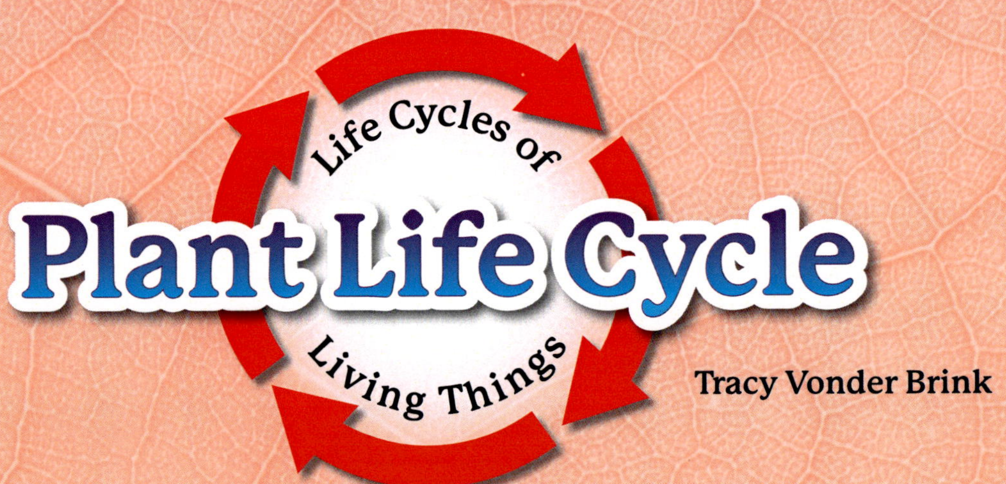

Tracy Vonder Brink

Table of Contents

A Starfish Book

Teaching Tips for Caregivers:

As a caregiver, you can help your child succeed in school by giving them a strong foundation in language and literacy skills and a desire to learn to read.

This book helps children grow by letting them practice reading skills.

Reading for pleasure and interest will help your child to develop reading skills and will give your child the opportunity to practice these skills in meaningful ways.

- Encourage your child to read on her own at home
- Encourage your child to practice reading aloud
- Encourage activities that require reading
- Establish a reading time
- Talk with your child
- Give your child writing materials

Teaching Tips for Teachers:

Research shows that one of the best ways for students to learn a new topic is to read about it.

Before Reading

- Read the "Words to Know" and discuss the meaning of each word.
- Read the back cover to see what the book is about.

During Reading

- When a student gets to a word that is unknown, ask them to look at the rest of the sentence to find clues to help with the meaning of the unknown word.
- Ask the student to write down any pages of the book that were confusing to them.

After Reading

- Discuss the main idea of the book.
- Ask students to give one detail that they learned in the book by showing a text dependent answer from the book.

Plant Life Cycle

All living things are born.

They grow to be adults.

We call these changes a life cycle.

Plants are living things.

They grow in soil.

Flowering plants have roots, **stems**, and leaves.

Stems hold the plant up and carry water and food from the roots to the leaves.

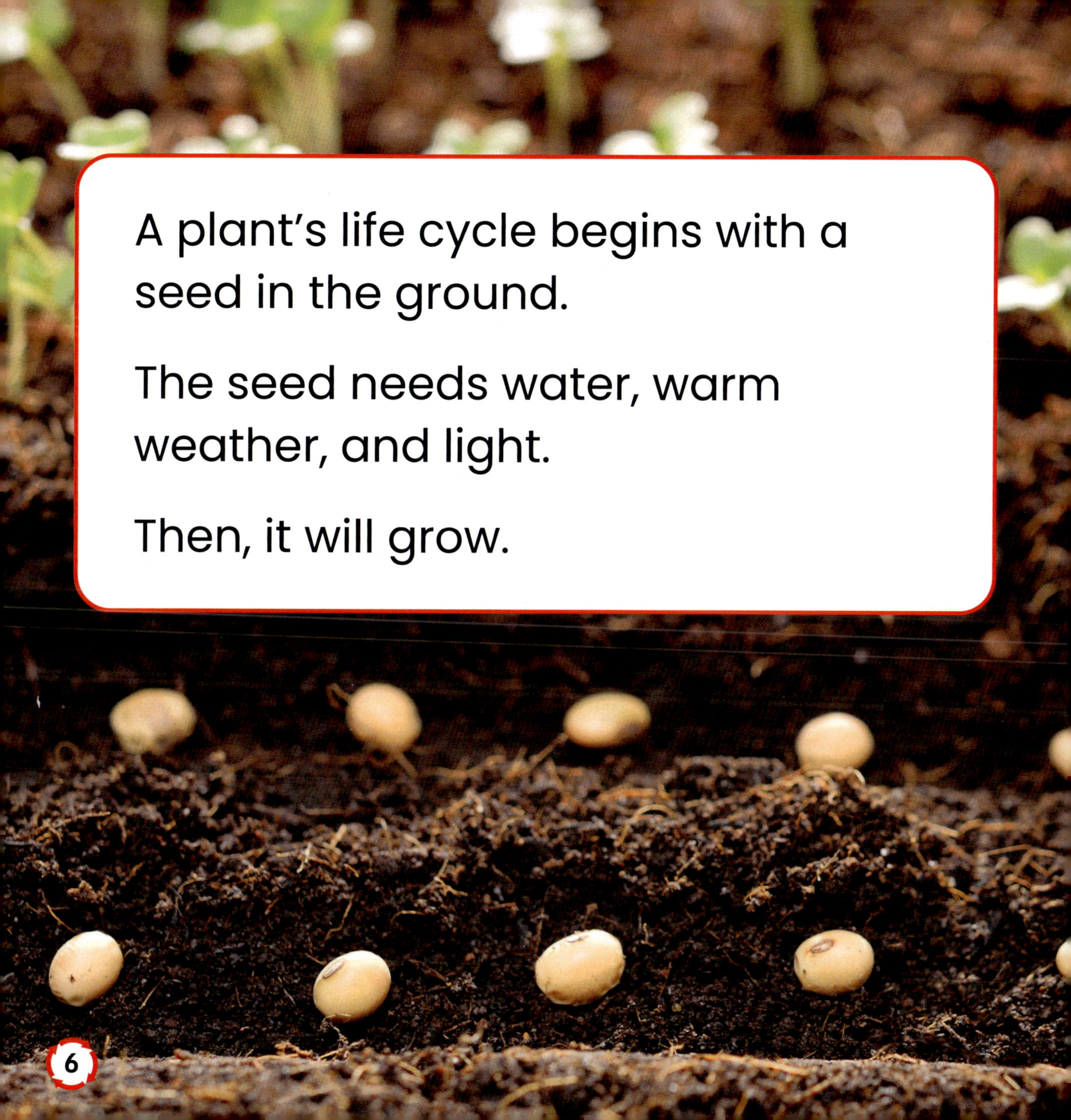

A plant's life cycle begins with a seed in the ground.

The seed needs water, warm weather, and light.

Then, it will grow.

The seed opens.

Roots and a **shoot** come out.

We call this **germination**.

A plant's roots keep growing its whole life.

Roots grow down and soak up **nutrients**.

The shoot pushes up out of the ground.

It makes leaves.

A plant using sunlight to make food is called photosynthesis.

The **seedling** uses sunlight to make food.

It also uses nutrients from its roots.

The young plant grows.

The young plant becomes an adult.

It makes flowers.

Flowers make **pollen**.

Flowers are brightly colored to attract bees and other creatures.

Bees and other creatures carrying pollen between plants is called pollination.

Pollen sticks to bees, birds, and other creatures that touch the flower.

They carry the pollen to another flower.

The flower uses pollen to make new seeds.

Some seeds grow inside fruit.

Some seeds fall from the plant.

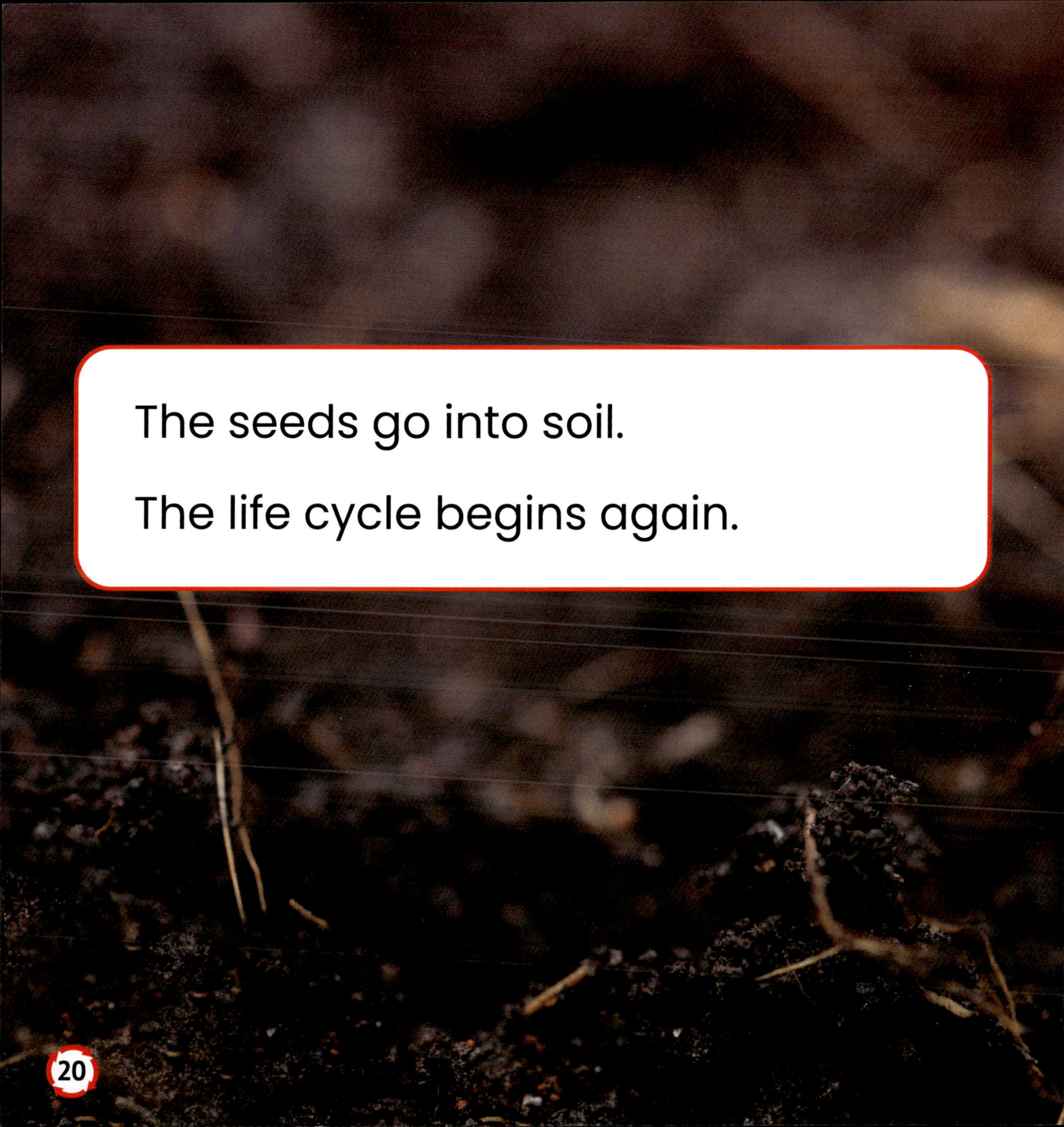

The seeds go into soil.

The life cycle begins again.

Words to Know

germination (jur-muh-NAY-shuhn): the development of a plant from a seed

nutrients (NOO-tree-uhnts): materials, such as minerals or vitamins, that are needed for healthy growth

pollen (PAH-luhn): fine, powdery grains produced by a flower

seedling (SEED-ling): a young plant grown from a seed

shoot (shoot): new growth of a plant

stems (stemz): the main, upward-growing parts of plants from which the leaves and flowers grow

Index

Comprehension Questions

1. A plant's life cycle begins with
a. an egg. **b.** a shoot. **c.** a seed.

2. A seedling uses ________ to make food.
a. pollen **b.** sunlight **c.** soil

3. A fl wer uses ________ to make seeds.
a. pollen
b. soil
c. bees

4. **True or false:** Seeds need water, warm weather, and light to grow.

5. **True or false:** Fruit does not contain seeds.

Answers
1. c 2. b 3. a 4. True 5. False

About the Author

Tracy Vonder Brink loves true stories and facts. She has written more than twenty books for kids and is a contributing editor for three children's science magazines. Tracy lives in Cincinnati, Ohio, with her husband, two daughters, and two rescue dogs.

Written by: Tracy Vonder Brink
Design by: Bobbie Houser
Editor: Kim Thompson
Production manager: Candice Campbell

Library of Congress PCN Data
Plant Life Cycle / Tracy Vonder Brink
Life Cycles of Living Things
ISBN 978-1-63897-457-4 (hard cover)
ISBN 978-1-63897-572-4 (paperback)
ISBN 978-1-63897-687-5 (EPUB)
ISBN 978-1-63897-802-2 (eBook)
Library of Congress Control Number: 2021953365

Printed in the U.S.A./CP052026

Photographs:
t = Top, b = Bottom, c = Center, l = Left, r = Right

Shutterstock: Barry Paterson: cover tl; Petrychenko Anton: cover tr; Mikael Damkier: cover b; Andrii Bezvershenko: p. 3; Filipe B. Varela: p. 5; amenic181: pp. 6-7; Anest: p. 9; showcake: p. 10; Romolo Tavani: pp. 12-13; Alexander Raths: pp. 14-15; Smeerjewegproducties: p. 16; Ekaterina Kondratova: p. 18; Foto2rich: pp. 20-21

Seahorse Publishing Company
www.seahorsepub.com

Published in the United States
Seahorse Publishing
PO Box 771325
Coral Springs, FL 33077